Ifeoma Onyefulu was born and brought up in eastern Nigeria.
After studying business management in London, she trained in photography
and then worked as a freelance press photographer. Her first book, *A is for Africa,*
was described by *Books for Keeps* as "like stepping from a darkened room straight into
noon sunshine". It was chosen by *Child Education* as one of the best information books
of 1993, and was selected for Children's Books of the Year 1994. Ifeoma has also
written *One Big Family, Chidi Only Likes Blue, Emeka's Gift* and *Ebele's Favourite,*
all for Frances Lincoln. She lives in London with her husband and two sons.

In memory of my grandfather, and for Chika Ekwensi

My Grandfather is a Magician copyright © Frances Lincoln Limited 1998
Text and illustrations copyright © Ifeoma Onyefulu 1998

First published in Great Britain in 1998 by Frances Lincoln Limited,
4 Torriano Mews, Torriano Avenue, London NW5 2RZ

First paperback edition 2000

The publishers would like to thank James Morley
of the Royal Botanic Gardens, Kew, and Dr H.M. Burkill, author of
The useful plants of tropical West Africa, (Royal Botanic Gardens, Kew, 1995)
for their help.

British Library Cataloguing in Publication Data available on request

ISBN 0-7112-1211-2 hardback
ISBN 0-7112-1342-9 paperback

Set in Stone Serif
Printed in China

5 7 9 8 6 4

*The treatments described in this book require thorough knowledge
and experience to prepare and administer. Many of the plants pictured
or referred to resemble other plants whose physiological effects may be
unpleasant or dangerous. Under no circumstances should any of the
treatments described in this book be attempted.*

My Grandfather is a Magician

Work and Wisdom in an African Village

IFEOMA ONYEFULU

FRANCES LINCOLN

Author's note

I am privileged to have had a grandfather, the late David Ekwensi, whose knowledge of plants, roots, tree-barks and animals was vast. He usually spent six months of the year in the forest hunting, and his survival there was largely due to the powers of plants and roots. One day he was bitten by a snake; what saved his life were the plant juices he rubbed into the bite and the roots he boiled and drank.

I remember my grandfather squeezing the juice out of a plant and giving it to my mother to drink, when she had stomach cramps. As a child, watching him at work was pure magic, but as I grew older, I realised it was not magic: his healing power came from the plants he used.

At Nkwelle Ezuaka, his village in eastern Nigeria, my grandfather helped many sick people, and was well-known as a healer. He was made a chief in recognition of his contribution to the village.

All over the world, the healing properties of plants, roots and tree-barks form the basis of traditional medicine. In Britain, people use dock leaves to relieve nettle-sting, while in Spain, aloe vera leaves bring relief to a sunburnt skin. However, the use of all plants, roots and tree-barks requires expert knowledge. Healing power tends to run in families, and valuable knowledge is passed down from generation to generation - although many people have now rejected traditional healing in favour of modern Western medicines.

I have written this book to keep alive the memory of my grandfather.

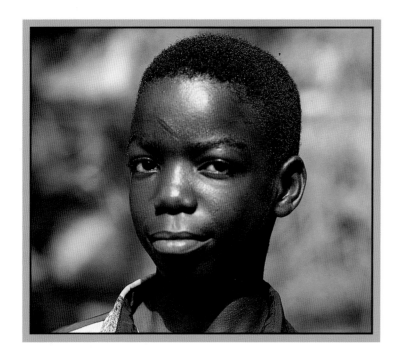

My grandfather is a magician. He uses leaves, roots and bark from trees and plants to help people who are ill or need help. Anyone with a problem can go to him for advice. People often say thank-you by giving him a goat or a chicken.

He is very special. Last year, when there was a big festival in my village, he stood up like a great tree and made a speech wishing them well. The clapping that greeted him sounded like thunder.

His work is different from everyone else's in my family. And we're a big family. Let me tell you about some of them.

My grandmother makes wedding gowns, party dresses and clothes for special occasions. She says it takes about two weeks to make a chief's robes, because she has to find special threads and buttons.

When she looks at the clothes she has made, her heart is filled with happiness.

But she is not as happy as Grandfather, when he is helping people.

My father teaches grown-ups in a big school. Later on, these grown-ups will teach children.

Here is my father at work. He is very clever - but Grandfather can still teach him a lot.

My mother owns a bakery. Here she is, buying flour and salt for baking bread. She has five bakers to make and bake the bread.

Her bread is delicious! People come in every day to buy it.

Here are my mother and two of her bakers, packing loaves into bags.

My mother works hard at home, too - I think she has magic powers! But Grandfather is more powerful than her because, even though he is 80, he is still working.

My uncle carves things out of wood. Great-grandfather taught him how to make wooden masks, dolls and animals when he was a little boy. People often send my uncle photographs of things they want him to make. Today he is carving antelopes.

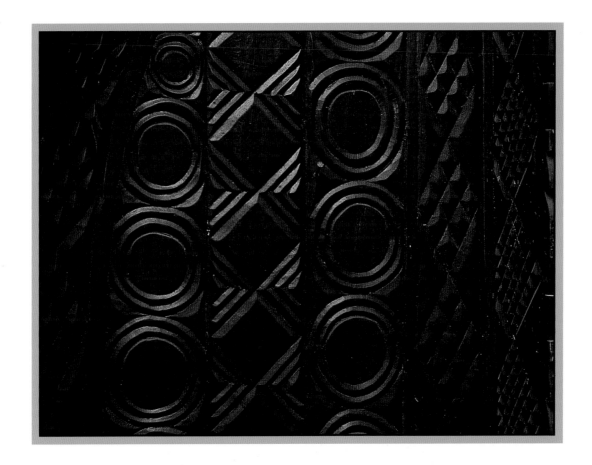

My uncle can make almost anything out of wood. Last week he carved a door for the chief of our village, and this is what it looked like.

He loves his work - but not as much as Grandfather does.

Uncle Law (that's what everyone calls him) has to wear these funny-looking clothes when he goes to work at a place called the High Court. I think the clothes make him look like a giant.

When someone is in trouble, Uncle Law stands up and speaks for them in Court. He really cares about people - but Grandfather cares even more.

This is my favourite auntie, who makes pots. She collects clay from the river-bank in our village. Then she starts to mould a small lump of clay, turning it round and adding more and more clay as she forms the shape.

Here she is, taking pots out of the fire after drying them out. My auntie knows a lot about earth and clay - but Grandfather knows even more.

My favourite uncle makes things out of iron. He melts the iron in the fire, and before it cools, he quickly beats it into the shape he wants with a heavy hammer. Sometimes he makes knives, keys and other things too. Here he is, pumping his bellows to make a fire.

And here he is, holding a hoe he has made. My uncle says it can be hard work, and that is why young people do not want to do this kind of work any more. One day, there will be no more blacksmiths in our family.

My uncle is strong - but Grandfather is stronger.

Auntie Ngo is a doctor.
She knows about all kinds
of illness because she
studied them for seven
years. Now she helps
people, especially women,
get better - but in different
ways from Grandfather.

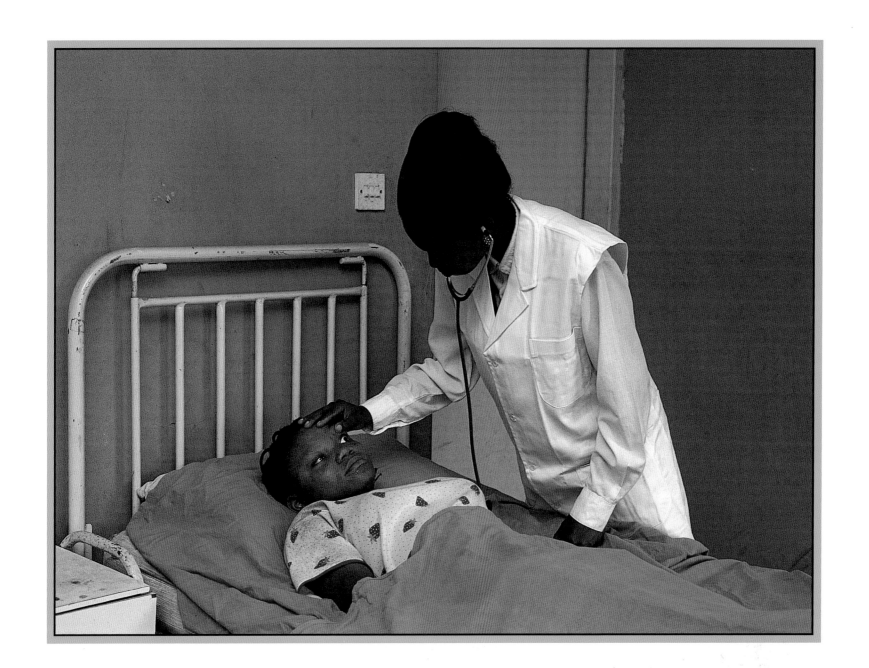

Yesterday I went to see Grandfather. He was healing a patient's leg. He used leaves to clean it, then rubbed in a herb mixture.

Afterwards, I said to him, "Grandfather, you are a magician. I know you are."

He smiled, "What makes you say that, child?"

"You know a lot about plants. And you walk many miles into the forest to collect them. That is magic!"

Grandfather shook his head.

"No, child." He picked up his staff. "Look - this staff is special. It shows I am only a messenger. I carry healing messages to sick people.

When I was small like you, my grandmother took me into the forest, and taught me about the powers of plants and trees. She told me to pick only what I needed, and not to waste anything. Plants and trees are very important to us, to the animals, and to the whole world. Sometimes we forget how special they are."

"Now," Grandfather said, "I want you to use your ears, eyes, and nose, because I am going to show you some of the powers of plants and trees. But remember, you must not use any of these, because you are still a child. I waited until I was 35 years old and had learnt a lot more about healing before I started to use them on patients."

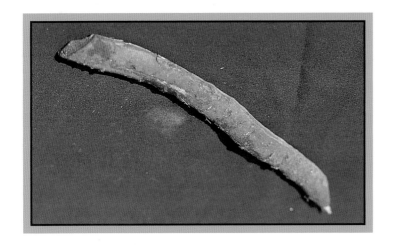

He pointed to a root,
    "We call this *okpokolo*. When the
root is boiled in water and the juice
is drunk, it brings down a fever.

Osencha is what we call this root.
    We boil it and use the juice to
        treat chest and hip pains.

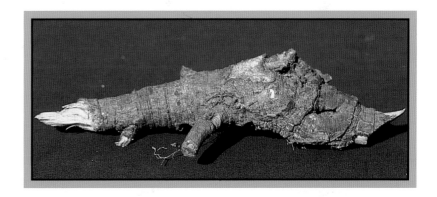

We call this plant *nsi ebilibi*.
We squeeze the juice from the leaves,
mix it with a little water and give it
as a drink to stop stomach pains."

Then Grandfather pointed to a small tree.

"This is called *dogoyaro*. This one is still a young tree, but it will grow much bigger. We squeeze the leaves into a little water and use the liquid to treat malaria, which is caused by mosquito bites. If I give a sick person dogoyaro juice to drink several times a day, the fever usually flies away.

"But if it doesn't go, I would give the person a steaming pot of dogoyaro leaves and roots to inhale. I would put layers of cloth on top of him to make him sweat quickly, and leave him alone for about five minutes. Then I would strain the liquid from the pot into a bowl of cold water for him to wash in."

Grandfather looked at me with sad eyes. "But no one wants to drink dogoyaro any more."

"Why not, Grandfather?" I asked.

"Everything is changing. No one likes to drink medicine unless it is sweet. And only a few people want to go into the forest or climb trees to collect these precious roots and leaves. We want everything to happen very quickly nowadays. It breaks my heart."

"But Grandfather," I said, "I want to be like you, and know all the powers of plants and trees."

He smiled. "And do you really want to visit the forest to see where they grow?"

"Yes, Grandfather, I do."

He smiled again.

"My child, you have made an old man very happy. But you will have to study hard before you know what I know. Many plants look alike - and while some can be used as medicine, others are harmful.

Now I must go and get ready. I have to collect plants before nightfall - but we'll start tomorrow."

My eyes followed my grandfather as he walked swiftly up the road holding his big knife. He got smaller and smaller until he vanished out of sight.

Now my heart is beating very fast, because I can't wait to be walking up that road with my grandfather tomorrow.

A note about Grandfather's plants

Not long ago, little attention would have been paid to Grandfather's extraordinary knowledge of local plants; indeed, people may even have regarded him as a witch doctor. But in recent years, scientists looking for new ways to treat illnesses have begun to discover that many traditional folk medicines really work. Now, ethnobotany – the science of plants, people and culture – is very important, with scientists all over the world working together to gather information and analyse plant extracts, before many rare and valuable plants on our planet become extinct.

Two of Grandfather's plants have been identified by ethnobotanists:

Dogoyaro *(Azadirachta indica, Family: Meliaceae) has recently been shown to contain effective antimalarial compounds. In Asia, it is known as neem.*

Okpokolo *(Anthocleista djalensis, Family: Loganiaceae) is a plant all of whose parts are reported to be active pharmacologically, especially the root. It has been used in traditional West African medicine to treat many conditions.*

It has not yet been possible to identify **osencha** *and* **nsi ebilibi**. *All the plants and roots in this book were photographed in the local government area of Anambra, south-eastern Nigeria, and their names are given in Ntiange, one of the many dialects spoken by the Igbo tribe.*

MORE PICTURE BOOKS IN PAPERBACK BY IFEOMA ONYEFULU PUBLISHED BY FRANCES LINCOLN

EMEKA'S GIFT

Emeka sets off to visit his grandmother in the next village. He would like to buy her a
special present and on his way he looks at all kinds of things, from 6 beautiful beaded necklaces to
9 pestles and mortars. A stunningly photographed counting book, full of information about African life.
"The author is mainly a photographer and a brilliant one too. Out of her love for Nigeria she
has made this outstanding counting book." *Junior Bookshelf*

Suitable for National Curriculum Geography, Key Stages 1 and 2; English – Reading, Key Stages 1 and 2
Scottish Guidelines Environmental Studies, Levels B and C; English Language – Reading, Levels B and C; Talking and Listening, Level B

Also available in Big Book format

ISBN 0-7112-1255-4
ISBN 0-7112-1447-6

ONE BIG FAMILY

Here is a unique insight into African village life. One little girl tells how each member of her family,
from her brother who helps sweep clean the village *ilo*, to her grandfather with his words of wisdom,
contributes to the well-being and happiness of their village.
"This stunningly illustrated book glows with warmth, joy and family pride and is an important
and positive contribution to the study of Africa." *Junior Education*

Suitable for National Curriculum Geography, Key Stages 1 and 2; English – Reading Key Stages 1 and 2
Scottish Guidelines Environmental Studies – Understanding People and Places, Level C; English Language – Reading, Level C

ISBN 0-7112-1346-1

Frances Lincoln titles are available from all good bookshops.